Arias of a Rhapsodic Spirit

Arias of a Rhapsodic Spirit

Poems by

Davidson Garrett

Cover design by Shay Culligan
Cover photography by Mary Ann Caffery

ISBN: 978-1-952326-27-1

Kelsay Books
502 South 1040 East, A-119
American Fork, Utah, 84003

In Memory of Viola Brown Garrett
and Dorothy Davies Miller

my first creative muses

Acknowledgments

Grateful acknowledgment is made to the editors of the following publications in which some of these poems first appeared, sometimes in somewhat different versions and/or with different titles:

Big City Lit, Brownstone Poets of Brooklyn Anthology, Come Hear: Rainbow Book Fair Anthology, First Literary Review East, HIV Here and Now, Impossible Archetype, Marco Polo Arts Mag, Meta-Land: Poets of the Palisades Vol. 2, On the Verge: Poets of the Palisades Vol. 3, Rutherford Red Wheelbarrow Anthology, Volumes, 9, 10, 11, 12, Sensations Magazine, Sensations Magazine Supplements, 7, 8, 9, The Ekphrastic Review, The Wild Angels Poets and Writers Anthology at The Cathedral of Saint John the Divine, and Third Wednesday.

Many thanks to my teachers of poetry who have inspired and guided me over the years: Dean Kostos, Molly Peacock, and Mark Nowak.

Grateful to my friends and family who have given me encouragement, support, and creative inspiration, as I strive to perfect my artistic endeavors, especially: Roger Anderson, William Toner, Joseph Wisniewski, William Traylor, Lulu LoLo, Dan Evans, Warren Platt, Laura Giner Bair, John J. Trause, David Messineo, Joel Allegretti, Jim Klein, Nafty Cohen, Amy Barone, Joseph Christopher Molloy, Seth Goldman, John McDonagh Roxanne Hoffman, Karen Neuberg, Francine Witte, Mary Ann Caffery, Taylor Caffery, Cindy Sostchen-Hochman, Louis Spirito, Eugenie Spirito, Patricia Carragon, Sheldon Firstenberg, and members of the PEN Worker Writers School.

A big thank you to my sister, Mary Ann Caffery, for her beautiful cover photo.

Additional thanks to Karen Kelsay and her wonderful staff at Kelsay Books, for making this book a reality.

Contents

Part One

Southern Baroque

Born in a Soggy Hospital Room

What image can convey humidity?
Should I oil paint droplets of water
on a blank canvas? Or superimpose

a photograph of a teal-colored lake
on a picture of a newborn's forehead?
When asked if I possibly remember

anything about my actual birth,
whether true or not—I always say
the air, the Louisiana air; thick air

you could slice with a butcher knife.
I inhaled this moist nitrogen gas
in & out to sustain my fragile life—

mixed with particles of carbon dioxide
dripping with an overabundance
of H_2o, capable of creating

static electric vapors
to spark dramatic thunderstorms
flashing orange/gold lightning

tingling lanugo fuzz on my baby body
generating an inherent reverence
for the volatile atmosphere

conducting the languid tempo
of my infantile days. Yes—
the brutal humidity, my first memory.

A Pastime in a Town Where Nothing Ever Happened

In Memory of Fred Davidson Garrett

My Father and I spent Sunday afternoons
at the Shreveport Airport—watching planes
take off and land. Since I was not into
sports or guns, this weekly adventure
was a plan by my disenchanted Dad
to spend quality time—with a son
who loved dolls more than baseballs.

In 1957, there was a teeny terminal
on the edge of our Louisiana city.
I remember revolving glass doors
opening into an air-conditioned lobby
soothing us from the tropical humidity
of the racially segregated state
where I was born. Skipping down

a narrow passage to check-in counters—
I inhaled the smell of shiny waxed floors
mixing with the scent of Samsonite luggage.
Women wearing hats, alongside suited men
stood in line receiving boarding passes.
On rectangular benches, I found discarded
ones, to pretend I too—might fly away

like Peter Pan. Colorful travel posters
adorned walls with printed slogans:
Explore Miami Beach. Signs on water
fountains boldly read: *For Whites Only.*
Strolling through a rear exit, we climbed stairs
taking us to an outdoor observation deck.
In a clearing, a paved runway bordered

pine forests as far as the eye could see.
And then, we waited and waited and waited.
"Look Daddy, I see one coming!" A blimp-like
speck descended from the cloudless heavens.
"That's the Delta landing from Atlanta"
my father would yell. Soon, the blue-gray
DC-6 touched down, hitting the earth

as billows of smoke surrounded fat tires.
The aircraft with spinning propellers
proceeded toward us on the tarmac
heading for a gate to unload passengers.
I delighted in the mighty gusts of wind
fanning my face—as the airliner
twirled around to park and refuel.

Its rotating motors whimpered silent
and a crew rushed under the fuselage
to safely secure this man-made bird.
Aluminum steps unfolded like magic
from the rear oval-shaped door
as well-to-do Caucasians deplaned
confident and coiffured. The stewardess

saying her goodbyes, looked dapper
clad in cap and snappy uniform.
Having witnessed this aeronautical
creature before, Daddy and I knew
it would be about fifteen minutes
till this arrival lifted off for Dallas.
We scurried to the restaurant inside

to cool off and drink an iced cherry Coke.
Gulping with straws, the sugary syrup
bathed our throats before we raced out
to watch folks board this big-winged toy.
I dreamed someday I'd ascend into the sky.
And now, half-a-century after those
sweet excursions ceased, I'm plagued

by a terrible fear of flying. Panic
attacks strike me—when contemplating
jetting away. Haven't flown in nearly
thirty years. Perhaps, if I could time travel
to that quaint airfield from former decades,
clasp my dead father's disillusioned hand,
my terror might be miraculously healed.

I'll never know,
since the deceased only
visit our minds to decipher memories.
But, my father's quiet expression of love
comes whenever I sip
an iced cherry Coke
or view a silver jet soaring above.

The Mock Turtle & Me

Beautiful Soup, so rich and green
Waiting in a hot tureen!
Who for such dainties would not stoop?
Soup of the evening, beautiful Soup!
                              —Lewis Carroll

At eight-years-old, after surviving
the prim & proper Eisenhower fifties,
I found myself elated, joyous—
acting in a children's theater troupe,

an ambitious, pint-sized performer
born with drive & determination.
I became the Mock Turtle
for this amateur production

of the fantastical *Alice in Wonderland,*
a theatrical diversion
to enhance mundane days
living in an oppressive segregated city

nestled in the northwest corner
of Bible-thumping Louisiana.
My co-actors, southern accented
boys & girls, created timeless characters

Charles Dodgson's imagination invented—
decked out in bright dancing tights
fitted snugly under cartoon-like apparel,
a visual kaleidoscope of make-believe—

our escape from the redneck world
we were unfortunately destined to inhabit.
Weeks before, my devoted mother
constructed an elaborate tortoise costume

designed from her rhapsodic mind.
Nimble fingers lovingly sculpted
the hard Chelonian shell
using two yards of chicken wire

covered by canvas potato sacks
dyed chocolate-brown. This concoction
attached to a cinnamon-colored
female bathing suit

fronted by stitched squares
stuffed with fistfuls of foam rubber
to represent the turtle's belly—
giving it a padded reptilian look.

To complete my creature attire,
my legs stretched into gray leotards
embellishing tubby thighs
as my freckled face absorbed

gobs of green greasepaint
with thick mascara highlighting
wistful eyes—
evoking a portrait of melancholy.

In my entrance scene, with scuba diving
flippers cushioning flabby feet, I waddled
onto the stage to greet curious Alice
standing beside the winged Gryphon.

I planted myself firmly, dead center
under the spotlighted proscenium arch.
With practiced falsetto, I began my lament
in a dirge-like tempo mingled with sobs:

Soup Soup, Beautiful Soup. Beautiful Beautiful Soup.

And from that moment on, I've never returned to reality

Venus

Before dawn's first vermillion streak
I gaze upon you, hot mysterious planet;
naked eyes wax, adore your shimmering light
as tears of recollection
mirror far away sparkles
reflecting steamy clouds in swirling dance.
Bright beacon that once steered ships across seas—
a whitish gleam in the fading night sky,
white as a sheet, like a Klansman's robe
hanging in a closet: revealed to my tiny ears
through a grandfather's whispering keyhole.

Louisiana afternoon, 1961: the Venus Movie Theater
sucks kiddies out of parents' blue-collar hair;
a single dollar turns B flicks
into cheap baby sitters—hypnotizing
with *Frankenstein* or *Teenagers from Outer Space.*
Launched into another galaxy by the Spaceship Hollywood,
buckteeth faces munch buttered popcorn
fit for Boris Karloff, a king of horror, whose evil masks
etched in black & white, produce bloodcurdling screams
in the southern cinema: escape from segregated,
vacuum-packed neighborhoods, called home.

Jupiter & Saturn thrill though telescopic lenses
creating kaleidoscopic delights—
earning glamorous media spin from scientists.
But, you are a modest morning star Venus,
your name derived from the goddess of love—
inspiring pastel canvases & lyres. In early morn
you are approachable—hovering in the heavens,
minute next to our moon, you coruscate
confidently in your orbit. Earth's little sister
illuminating dignity: I yearn for your serene distance
millions of miles from memories of monstrous matinees.

My Two Grandfathers

Grandfather George, my father's father
died when I was five. A Germanic face
with owl eyes, an abstract of foreboding
residing in my mind's early snapshots.
A shrewd businessman for real estate—
he lived frugally in a wood framed house
on Fair Place. Frugal also in his love,
I never remember an embrace or hug.

Grandfather Herman, my mother's father—
a bald frog of a man, croaked when I turned
ten. Southern as a pine with Confederate
blood, his Methodist funeral, a refined
spectacle of scripture & wailing women
featured red-capped Shriners for pallbearers.
I recall this cigar smoker's penchant for cats
& how he pinched my arms for punishments.

The Day Kennedy Got Shot: Novmber 22, 1963

Claiborne Elementary School: Shreveport, Louisiana

Early Friday afternoon,
our sixth grade teacher, Mr. Waters,
assigns Peggy as monitor; instructs her

to jot down names on the chalkboard
if anyone leaves their seats. He hurriedly
exits the room—& the class goes wild

as only eleven-year-olds can do,
elated the teacher has ducked out
for an impromptu meeting. Tough boys

begin their bullying. Quiet girls pair up,
chat about weekend plans. Peggy threatens
us all, but no one listens to her. The air

is humid on this November day
& there are pictures of Pilgrims
on the bulletin board—since Thanksgiving

is next week. I daydream about
my bowling party tonight
with the Methodist Youth Fellowship.

Randy & John start cursing
at the top of their lungs. Sneaky
Madeline steals a pencil from Ann

ensuing a verbal fight.
Everyone takes sides. I'm bloated
from a fish sticks lunch

& lay my head on my desk
smelling newly mown grass
from an open window. The noise gets

louder, the children out-of-control.
Suddenly, Mr. Waters opens the door
surprising us all. We freeze in silence.

Glaring at us, he walks solemnly
& stands beneath the American flag
hanging above the name-filled chalkboard.

We know he'll give us homework
to punish us for bad behavior—
but instead, in a quavering voice

with watery eyes, he speaks
in a slow southern cadence:
"The President of the United States is Dead."

Eerie quiet. Some trashy boys
giggle, & Diane claps.Their parents
hated John Kennedy—since he believed

blacks were equal to whites.
Stunned, I wonder if I'll still go
to my bowling party this evening.

Hawaii the Film:1966

How utterly disappointing for me
the much heralded film—*Hawaii*
viewing it in downtown Denver
during my fourteenth summer. Great
Aunt Mattie Belle & I—had salivated
over Julie Andrews in *The Sound of Music*
a year before. We knew absolutely nothing
about James Michener's epic novel
this current spectacle was adapted from.
My senior citizen sidekick, envisioned
Maria von Trapp singing *Aloha 'Oe*
playing the ukulele in a grass skirt
after noticing the picture's advertisement
in *The Rocky Mountain News.* Inside
an Art Deco movie theater, our naïve eyes
popped-out when half-naked women
swam to greet a white-sailed schooner
docking in the Pacific—near Lahaina, Maui.
Max von Sydow, portrayed a 19th Century
minister, seeking to convert the heathens
to Christianity. Our dear British songbird
played his not-so-devoted wife—
gloomy, serious, heartbroken by unrequited
love. Warring natives, bloody childbirths,
graven image worship by island locals
plodded on for three hours, without any
music by Elvis—singing *Blue Hawaii.*
After the Panavision extravaganza ended,
my cinema seatmate decided
she could skip a trip to exotic Honolulu.
Returning home, we created our own
luau feast, devouring thick baked ham
sweetened by canned pineapple slices
& washed down with cold Hawaiian Punch.

Denver: Summer of 1969

I thought I knew everything
about everything. Little did I grasp—
I knew very little about anything.
A studious, sixteen-year-old
studying at a fancy university
for six intensive weeks—
floating on my first Cloud 9—
feeling like a free spirit, alone in a
rambunctious cow town
dripping with hippies.
Tie-dyed tank tops, waist length hair
festooned the Mile High City
during my glorious summer
of psychedelic awakening.
Everyone I encountered
appeared eighteen or younger—
strolling the avenues, smoking
cheap pot: rebelling, rebelling
rebelling! The Rocky Mountains
soaring: a perfect backdrop
for the amplified, celebration
of eternal youth. Led Zepplin
blared out of dashboard radios
from rusted vans
painted with flowers and peace signs.
Protesters, angered by Vietnam's
carnage, tangled narrow streets—
lustily chanting: "Make Love Not War."
And I was there, breathing in
all the rage, all the wondrous joy,

all the Whitmanesque
promise: my birthright
in our beloved—America.
I thought I knew everything
about everything. However,
my coming-of-age education
unfolded quite slowly, like a
delicate rose blissfully opening
amid the clamorous
cacophony, of a turbulent decade.

At Eighteen: London Saturday Noon

Sunshine, the color of strained tea
seeps through a sieve
of steel-gray sky, reflecting

burnished light
on the river Thames;
distant bells chime

beyond impressionistic
etchings of eaves
lining the banks

near Parliament.
Big Ben interrupts,
his massive voice

sounds like a Mussorgsky
basso. Once a faraway world,
now the very world

of my present.
Innocent desires manifest
from my romantic mind

seizing this British moment—
a moment of crimson epiphany
in a nascent lifespan,

a split second surge of
thought process, plotting
the thematic motifs

for the developing narrative.
Who? What? Where? Why?
O literary city

vibrant with scattered traces
of Dickensian imagery—
you promise no absolute answers

to a thespian-in-training—
merely tucked away questions
framing this midday so foreign.

As lingering fog evanesces
with aid by tenacious rays,
a solitary stroll rehearses

wild emotions
in my own histrionic drama
analyzed by internal monologues

destined to be filed under
Awakenings, in memory's
cluttered cabinet.

At Three, a drawing room
matinee, sugar cake fluff
digesting into starless night,

a dot on my evolving timeline,
a bold-inked dot,
where, in mystical reverie

I will return again and again
until the radiant curtain
of death, slowly descends.

The Night Before Christmas Eve: Germany, 1970

For Leslie Conerly Lolley

Advent darkness. Determined stars sneak through
tiny breaks of swirling cloud cover, hovering over
West Berlin. A walled city, decorated with simple
holly & greens, unwilling to sanction holiday

overkill during chilled rhetoric of Cold War.
Two eighteen-year-olds from Louisiana,
a closeted homosexual & a Carol Burnett *wannabe*—
actors on a college sponsored USO tour,

rejoice in their new found freedom; adolescent troubles
frozen till January's return. Chance or misfortune
conducts this performance of youth's final cabaletta.
Burning the pocket of the young male, tickets for

the Deutsche Opera's traditionally staged *Tosca.*
Navigating through mink coats & men in leather,
the bug-eyed hicks climb to the nosebleed section
of a surprisingly modern theater. As the soprano

finishes her aria, *Vissi d'arte,* the enthusiastic
Americans scream, "Brava Diva!" Foreign commentary
scorned by German etiquette—as gruff voices declare:
"heathens im haus"—erupting belly laughter heard

far beyond barbed wire. A swift curtain call escape.
Puccini's lyrical drama—fuels ravenous appetites,
strolling along the Kurfürstendamm, past the historic
Kaiser-Wilhelm-Gedächtniskirche, its bombed steeple

a reminder of the horrors of World War II
nestled in the sliced heart of an occupied metropolis.
Signs on café after café read: *Geschlossen.* Weary limbs,
growling stomachs—until a neon Kris Kringle glows

above an open beer garden. Steak, sausage,
schnitzel, sauerbraten, potatoes & ice cream:
the first course gobbled near the stroke of 2 a.m.
Afterward, a Mercedes taxi driven by a native

with a broken compass—delivers Hansel & Gretel
to an aluminum dormitory, courtesy of the U.S. Army.
On this stark night, friendship's fleeting light
will be transformed into a sweet operatic memory.

A Yuletide gift for the songless years to come.

Part Two

Dramatic Coloratura

Killer Bronchitis

Gross gunk, bronchial phlegm
coughed up through a blocked wind pipe
spouting like a green geyser. Enough combustion
to bust ribs & stretch elastic muscles—

a walking misery—fueling a fear of death,
a masked death
lurking silently, in gray shifting shadows—
reminding the body

life is as fragile as a breezy sneeze.
Moment by moment survival
never ever guaranteed
while precious breaths

wheeze out of inflamed nostrils
& I contemplate—self-perceived maculations—
blaming questionable behavior
for an inconvenient illness

exacerbated by routine negligence
of my fleshy temple. Fiercely driven
by visions of high-powered living,
a daily existence—conjuring stress

in every conceivable fashion—
I bargain for the Lord's mercy
one last time, if by chance
I miraculously receive: instantaneous healing.

Almighty Creator, please make me well, and I promise that...

The Clutter of Creation

I live in the clutter of creation
with heaps of papers piled on my desk:
a mountainous mélange of first drafts
being saved for future reference
in case a jeweled phrase abounds.
Books on the floor—stacked like skyscrapers
held upright by foundations of knowledge
hide collected dust on the rug
that's blown inside from one window
to the world—which allows sunbeams
splashing through a dirty pane of glass
affirming light will always penetrate
the dark & triumph. Cassette recordings
in every nook of the humble home—
create a soundtrack of mystical music
to transcend hopeless housekeeping habits
blessing the air with halcyon sounds
that inspire me, a passionate urban monk
striving to bring Augustine order
to superfluous words on the page
by tidying up my poems, which someday
still might endure—long after
the messy cell is buried in earth's core—
forgotten along with diurnal duties
of cleaning the stark living space.

Polishing the soul's real treasures
must always take precedence
over the task of rearranging
disposable transient objects.

Forty Pounds Counting

Hot cinnamon rolls seduce my nostrils
strolling into your bustling bakery
perfumed by flavored coffees & herb teas.
With you manning the counter, I'm thrilled
to admire your sensuous self, filling
white boxes with huge cannoli. Eyes see
delectable deserts: fruit tarts, Whoopie
pies, a fattening assortment—to kill
my diet. Yet, I'll forgo losing weight—
buttering-you-up with sales, future mate.
(In my dreams.) I swoon, staring at your buns
each day, purchasing sugared confections.
Wolfing éclairs to please you, I down tons
of whipped cream, bulging for your affection.

The Bathhouse: A Sestina in B Natural

Towels wrapped around waists of hard torsos,
half-nude men swagger through darkened halls
concealing their prized penises—
seeking relief for sexual frustration
interwoven with repressed guilt & fears
while HIV lurks, threatening the game.

Strangers cruise in a sensuous game,
roaming eyes gaze at buffed torsos—
steroid-pumped torsos full of queer fears
gathering in a maze of narrow halls
scented by poppers. Succor for frustration
while couples pair off to worship penises

in a market place stocked with penises
devoid of rules dictating the game.
An escape for closeted frustrations
with plenty of big rippled torsos
massed safely together in eerie halls
retreating from deep-rooted boyhood fears.

Years of amplified homophobic fears
by preachers damning acts of penises
echo like screaming ghosts in steamy halls
haunting players in this erotic game
as smug narcissists lure torsos
begging a quick fix for carnal frustrations.

Midnight approaches, pent-up frustrations
are drugged by crystal & coke; ever fearful
arms enfold around perspiring torsos
as lucky mouths suck erect penises
inside cubicles. Scoring in the game—
exploding orgasms rumble the halls.

At dawn, the anonymous halls
greet a fresh batch of homos—frustrated,
allowing a new team for the sex game
to mollify suppressed religious fears.
Roving hands jerk agreeable penises
dangling from the groins of tender torsos.

Biblical fears of penises
created this torso-hunting game
in grim halls pacifying lifelong frustrations.

Musical Glue

In Memory of Thomas Patrick Savage

On the Great Lawn in Central Park
canopied by a steamy summer sky,
you & I recline blanket to blanket
till sunset's glow—psyched up
for Fiorenza Cossotto as Carmen
with the Metropolitan Opera—alfresco.
We are young & our eyes sparkle
with far-flung expectations—
we think the diva's face out of Goya,
delighted by her grand gesticulations
as dreams rustle under sways of ginkgos.
The flirting gypsy wears a Spanish mantilla
organdy roses in her cleavage,
she clicks castanets in a crimson dress
madly dancing a sexy seguidilla.
How we scream for endless encores
adoring this monumental mezzo—
her eyes gleam at the lusty bravas
from the vociferous gay matadors.

But now, my classical music comrade,
you are dead from cruel AIDS
as you flamenco through
air & wind. Only memory sends back
that Habanera sung beneath moonbeams
with a chesty register break
jolting like a San Francisco quake.
O Toreador, dear sweet Toreador,
I'll forever remember the way
our operatic friendship tightly bonded
listening to arias by Bizet.

Intimacy Problems

I spot my bipolar boyfriend, who claims
he once catered with Martha Stewart,
browsing in Delectable Delicacies
on fashionable Fifth Avenue. Well—

not exactly the fashionable part,
that shady strip shadowed by
The Flatiron, where homeless men
gather near Madison Square, to compare

stories of distress & deprivation.
I glance from behind the coffee counter,
hear him banter with a Korean cashier,
this former culinary chef—seemingly

recuperated from his winter doldrums
of fear. They say spring is a natural healer,
but let's face it, if I had a good excuse
like certified mental illness, I might have

vegetated during winter days of gloom
under covers on a futon too.
I used to deliver him lunch
to his subsidized flat, squeezing

sandwiches into passive hands
through a chained door crack.
This became a thankless
bore-of-a-chore. Still, I prayed

the handsome food wizard—
who often crawled on his knees
to receive these edible gifts—
might one day rise triumphantly

43

like Lazarus, exorcise his inner
demons, be permanently cured
from this psychosis—alternating
between mania & melancholia.

On one occasion, Campbell's Chunky
exchanged into shaky fingers
from mine, triggering loony bin
chaos. The medicated cook

whacked the wooden barrier shut
primal screaming from behind—
"STAY FAR AWAY,"
a terrifying symptom of

mood swinging madness.
Alas, the needy masochist
that I am, kept returning
as if a fierce cat who scratched

might forgive & forget.
Fierce cats don't. Mister Doom
banished me forever
from his kingdom of darkness.

And now, I witness a miracle.
My mercurial gentleman
salivates over imported cheese
like a chic hostess buying goodies

for an impromptu picnic.
On this clear day, despite
my grated feelings, I'm happy
his psychological resurrection

inspires gourmet gawking,
or perhaps even a smile
at a cruising customer
wandering the aisles

until he realizes—it's me.

Il Fantasma: Living at the McBurney YMCA,
   1985

Like Mad Lucia di Lammermoor
I wander eerie halls in stark darkness

not in a bloody wedding gown—
but tiptoeing, wrapped in a white towel.

Overwrought Lucia—murdered her husband
because of a forced unwanted nuptial.

My marriage to my art, paralyzed by fear
from a virus looming in a metropolis of death.

Despair, disease, all around—
festering in a nightmare house of reclusive souls.

The AIDS plague of New York City
zaps my neighbors—creating emaciated faces

of horror. Crazy Lucy heard internal voices
as I hear woeful men moaning

minor key shrieks behind closed doors.
The phantasmagoric voices in my head

plead—do not give up and die—
keep plodding an unbroken legato line.

For within these operatic walls of doom
a seed of harmonious bliss may soon be planted.

In the Jury Duty Waiting Room

Cross-examining myself
like a two-bit lawyer
in an open & shut case—
I plead guilty
to the Almighty Universe,
confessing to self-perceived
offenses. Rage & perplexity
erupt like mini-tempests
battering a half-crazed mind
decorated with fading memorabilia.
Memorabilia, to constantly remind
my traumatized soul—of its youthful yearnings
withering in psychotic paralysis—
numbing the spontaneity
of creativity
like a stroke attacking the brain
with unapologetic surprise. Did I create
this mental mishmash (as suggested
by New Age gurus
proselytizing for acolytes?)

Nursery rhymes, only nursery rhymes
do justice to disjointed questions—
laughing myself into wild hysterics
at the dribble of my fractured—*what ifs?*

Advent Purple: December, 1989

For Paul Michael Fontana

Today we will go on a field trip. First,
The Cathedral of Saint John the Divine,
afterward—across frozen Central Park
to New York's crown jewel,

The Metropolitan Museum of Art—
its Yule tree with hand-carved cherubs
our grand finale. Thirty—seven-year-olds
must be bundled for icy swirls of wind.

A bus stop, an eternal wait, a subway
& a walk—bring us to the Gothic temple
standing like a fortress near Harlem's border.
Hyped up children adore the peace park

with its animals sculpted in iron—
juxtaposed to gray unfinished towers.
Once inside the church of the bishop,
joy turns sullen. In small groups

we wander along the nave
of the stained glass structure
dedicated to the saint—whose revelations
prophesied the impending Battle of Armageddon.

A girl complains, "I'm bored." Her chaperone
mother laments, "My daughter needs to eat."
Copycat sentiments echo through marble
chapels, like falling dominoes. Our schedule

precludes fast food. Having escaped
the misunderstood world of the South Bronx
I think to myself: *Why can't we enjoy beauty
instead of French fries just once?* Onward—

we trudge eastward, like the Magi
following Bethlehem's star. With frigid feet
we reach Fifth Avenue's noble shrine of art
that documents civilization. Beneath an

ivory veil of swirling snowflakes,
ebony legs rush up slushy steps
pushing past tourists dressed
in seasonal best. With reluctance,

the scowling contribution collector
accepts our meager offering of coins.
"I don't wanna go," a whiny voice cries.
"Me neither," a chorus of tired angels sing.

December magic doesn't cast its spell,
the medieval gallery's Neapolitan crèche
can't raise an "Ah." Time to depart
back into the beige of urban reality.

Fragile beings snared by the pallor
of poverty, & a teacher who wonders
if far-fetched dreams ever crystallize—
solemnly plod toward the steel train

that will clack us back
to dilapidated buildings, remnants of
decay, in the heart of drug territory.
At school, chicken spaghetti steams,

the hungry dears are fed.
Christmas expectations disappear
into the walls of a Catholic cafeteria.
Noel. Noel.

Part Three

Lyric Baritone

After Death

Anne Evans Point Overlooking Mount Evans

Under burnt gold aspens
my newly blessed ashes
placed, emancipated from
man-made sins, sealed inside

an urn, buried, laced by blue
columbines of Colorado.
My spirit awaits
a non-theological taste

of the divine. In virgin days
I escaped for summer respite
(a wide-eyed adolescent)
to this hallowed spot—

wishful, aglow
with thespian dreams
of bright, iridescent lights
illuminating marquees

on Broadway. Reveling
at the slithered crescent moon
rising above an etched gray
outline of Rocky Mountains—

I dozed beneath stars
till break of day
flooded me
with dazzling strains

of sunbursts, painting wildflowers
in orange and magenta, grass stains
soaked into crumpled slacks.
My heart rushed madly

awakening to youthful possibilities
witnessing new found heaven—
blushed with promise. The alpine
breeze blowing on innocent skin

prompted me to gleefully sing
an aria, pinching my forearm
to seize the day. An actor's life
did not bring wealth or fame,

but grimy urban gloom—
now, only wistful memories
cling to the cerulean sky
hovering over my natural tomb

as I rest peacefully in Mother Earth's womb.

After *Traviata*

no one speaks,
the silent congregation
files out of the temple of music

like high-toned peacocks
into the winter slush. Iced urbanites
flee underground to subway platforms,

thumb through half-read programs—
using the glossy booklets as blinders
to avoid eye contact with fellow Verdians.

Even Violetta's checkered life,
a French courtesan, can't evoke a scandalous word
from the patrons of art

returning to reality, cultured neurotics.
Surely some opera queen hated the soprano's
tendency to pinch the pitch,

or the tenor's struggle
hitting a home run high C.
Have any of these vocal fanatics

torn out their heart from fornicated-flesh
and presented it to their lover on numbed knees?
Whatever thoughts bubble into these bel canto brains,

they are kept locked inside
emotional chests of solitude
all the ornamented passion of *Sempre libera*

will never open, as clacking trains depart
and the tight-lipped buffs
fade into tunnels of darkness.

Heart & Flowers

In the summer of 1954, my Great Aunt Mattie Belle
arranged flowers for Jeanette MacDonald—
handcrafted petite bouquets

for tossing over footlights
at the end of the movie star's concert
in Colorado's Red Rocks, an amphitheater sculpted by nature

from glacial stone. Pink carnations & purple columbines
bound by silver & gold streamers
made each floral tribute—fragrant jewels

befitting the Hollywood queen. A lump-of-a-woman
with a limp, Auntie Matt drove a beat-up station wagon
into hills above dusky Denver, presented the scented gifts

to ushers at the entrance door, requesting blossom-showers
be thrown after final encores. Grandmother's baby sister
returned to the parking lot, sat in still solitude

on auto's tailgate, listening to the faint songbird
chirping beneath a twinkling Rocky Mountain sky.
Next day's newspaper, pictured America's singing sweetheart

clenching the love offerings—above a critic's rave.
Alone, in a steamy greenhouse, pruning her fractured roses,
the anonymous admirer hummed in transcendent reverie—

Ah Sweet Mystery of Life, at Last I've Found Thee.

Doctor Gioachino's Remedy (For the Blues)

A dose of Rossini guarantees to make you gay
when life's vicissitudes become a bitter pill—
listen to *La Donna del Lago*—at least once a day.

Make sure the recording is with Montserrat Caballé
or try a bubbling elixir—*The Barber of Seville*—
a prescription of Rossini guarantees you'll be gay.

For deep depression—meditate upon *Semiramide;*
there's healing balm hearing Joan Sutherland's trill—
& listen to *La Donna del Lago*—every waking day.

Armida—by the hour, with Callas having her say,
salubrious joy through your heart will fill—
Rossini's roulades guarantee to make you gay.

William Tell's apple keeps the doctor away
as Lone Ranger's theme shoots the blues to kill—
dance wildly to *La Donna del Lago* every gay day!

Tancredi's coloratura crushes quotidian dismay
& *The Siege of Corinth* battles scales that thrill—
a dose of Rossini guarantees to make you gay
if you listen to *La Donna del Lago*—at least once a day.

Gioachino Rossini—1792-1868

Sensations Magazine Reading in Old Lafayette Village

In Memory of Kleber de Freitas

1

some poets gather
on a summer afternoon
under a covered bridge
to recite eclectic poems
as a brook babbles beneath

2

four picnic tables
with matching benches of wood
seat serious scribes
who munch homemade sandwiches
& gulp coffee, tea, & pop

3

a Brazilian
clutches an old camcorder
to record moments
for future posterity
the publisher will archive

4

resolute women
voice smart sonnets andante
accompanied by
bird chirping & traffic sounds
as all attendees swat flies

5

men howl heated verse
cooled by refreshing breezes
as poetic words
become a rhythmic music
mingling with rustling green leaves

6

a community
bonds by nature & language
in sweet fellowship
to stimulate each one's muse
forever through memories

Manhattan Kundry with Dry Eye Syndrome

Yellowish juice
oozes over corneas,

translucent slush stagnates
under lids: creates painful viewing

of winter snow
rotting on empty streets

of a refrigerated city.
If only I could see clearly

out of these eyes
weeping tears sticky as glue,

I might witness the face
of my Parsifal

leaping past The Flatiron
or mirrored—by the redemptive glow

of Chrysler's spire. For today, I must settle
for blurred vision, as seasonal illness

distracts me from a heroic love
appearing only in shadows of stone.

Dame Gwyneth

For Dame Gwyneth Jones

Steadfast daughter of the gods,
stentorian soprano, born in Wales—
you have been kissed by the music of Strauss,
tempered with integrity by Wagner's pen,
a paragon for symphonic spirits—
defying bitter critics
with an iron will of divine trust
as you genuflect to destiny,
breathing life into listless libretti—
blessing musical scores with dramatic flesh and blood—
allowing no being to jolt your earthly visit
as the incarnation of Art.

Zoo Ballet

Madame Ostrich pliés like Margot Fonteyn
in sweet prime. Snubbing a rapt audience
gawking from behind a chain-link fence—
the fowl ballerina jetés. Fans crane
necks to view her natural, no nonsense
approach to dance. Lithe, breezy, rainbow glints
of sun spotlight the bird, now quite insane.
Out of African habitat, resigned
to confinement, she's scrambled her own mind.
Detached arabesques in stark solitude—
this mad Struthio evokes regal bearing.
Whirling pirouettes earn hand-thrown food
into her prison, by humans staring.

The Wine Salesman

On the city sidewalk, raindrops
pelt his new penny loafers. Late

for a client meeting, a woman
brushes his soaked hair

with her bulky umbrella. Still,
the tuna sandwich

he hastily gobbles
dodging splashy puddles

satisfies more
than any aged Chardonnay.

Ellen Terry Speaks Frankly to John Singer Sargent:1889

And why the insistent rush to paint me
as Lady Macbeth? You see kind artist,
a portrait is forever. I will list
my reluctance with the names of three:
Beatrice, Viola, and mad Ophelia.
These Shakespearian roles, all steadfast
hearts, my public expects that I'll be cast.
And critics proclaim: "She shines as Portia."
I'm conflicted over whether I've got
enough evil within to portray the Scot?
Give me time to let this part congeal
while I plot murder for King Duncan's crown.
If I assess a triumph, I'll make a deal:
I'll pose for you in my beetle-winged gown.

* Ellen Terry did triumph as Lady Macbeth in December,1888 at the Lyceum Theatre in London. She performed the role 150 times to sold-out audiences. After her success, she agreed to have her portrait painted.

Coney Island Forever

Saturday I spent at Coney Island...
—Walt Whitman

1

Humanity clings
to a brownish sand carpet
on Atlantic's shore
while flesh tans in bikinis
& dreamers muse under sky.

2

Brooklyn's famous beach
creates mental harmony
with its storied past
which inspired great poetry
from the pen of Walt Whitman.

3

Sigmund Freud popped by
in 1909, to view
the grand amusements:
Steeplechase Park, Luna Park
& of course, surreal Dreamland.

4

New Yorkers still flock
to the ocean's healing balm
away from urban strife
mingling in tranquility
amid throngs of diversity.

5

An ice cold green sea
surprises dainty tootsies
when putting nude feet
into chilled salty water
& screaming with joyful glee.

6

Must we ever leave
our blessed Coney Island
& sadly return
back to reality's stress
from our outing of sweet peace.

Sun and Shadows

1

Saffron sun blinds eyes
walking easterly forenoon.
Under a building's
shadow, I briefly pause, don
overblown, Jackie O shades.

2

Trees casting shadows
and a hammock invite me
to lie down in peace.
An intrusive sun invades
through insouciant branches.

3

Is heaven framed by
golden sunlight? I wonder
if Satan's shadow
sneaks beyond St. Peter's gate?
No. Shadowy figures banned.

4

You, a sun god, when
I fell love-crazy for your
sparkle. But alas,
the mythic hero I sensed,
just a sadistic shadow.

5

Peter Pan's shadow
detached on television.
In childhood, it shocked.
Mary Martin's radiance
calmed. Her face, beams of sunshine.

The Ascension

As he said this, he was lifted up while they looked on,
and a cloud took him from their sight...
—The Acts of the Apostles: 1:9

Into ashen sky
I rise upward
bright as sunshine

dazzling from afar;
scarred body of flesh
evanesces, becoming

sparking mist
illuminating cloud cover.
My mystical farewell

overwhelms minds
of devoted acolytes—
faithful followers

deciphering their heart's
ineffable stirrings.
A phantasmagoric

metaphysical shift,
witnessed in awe
by truth seekers

unable to fully comprehend
my final transformation
from man to eternal spirit.

My Artistic Trade Off

What will my poetic mind sing to me?
Nestled in my cheap abode, I admire
through glass—the Empire State Building's spire
glistening with majestic dignity.
Luckily, a daily view, this stalwart gem
a soothing neighbor, as I accept my fate
of hand-to-mouth poverty. Contemplating
my bare bones life, it's really not so grim.
After all, I live in Manhattan's heart
where tourists sightsee in T-shirted droves
tasting a bite of the dazzling Big Apple
as they flee Boise, Des Moines or Detroit.
City life, a rousing muse, with large troves
of urban lore—for my brain's scribe to grapple.

On Fifth Avenue in Summer

hordes of
entitled millennials
wear frown faces
clogging the sidewalk
lost in ghostlike
trances
glued to handheld
devices
entertaining
engaged eyes
as growling traffic
whizzes by
creating massive
congestion
with shrieking horns
blaring *honk honk honk*
becoming a background
soundtrack
never distracting
this fierce onslaught
of muscled legs
& Equinox butts
stomping beneath
glassy skyscrapers
grappling
narcissistic agendas
completely unaware
of every other
robotic body

engulfed
with individualistic
fury—as each wonders
what happened
after awakening
when pastel dreams
morphed into
workaday misery
with no breakfast
at Tiffany's
while the blazing sun
bakes cracked concrete
burning dissatisfied feet

In a Community Garden on West 111th Street

In Memory of Lola Dunn

I envision your luminous presence
swirling into my mind's blank universe
amid falling leaves & metallic chairs.
Wrapping tightly around my autumnal heart
like a silk shroud of love, your ghostly spirit
embraces the enigmatic stillness
of this lonely leftover. I nimbly stroll
hearing faint music from the whistling breeze
as each step recreates a rhythmic scat—
& you tickle my fancy with chansons
of not-so-long-ago, when you jammed like
Billie Holiday in this sweet oasis
fragrant with lilacs & roses. You threatened
to spend eternity tending their fragile blooms.

The Second Day of January: Ice Water in the Face

After the holidays, reality jolts
one into Freudian introspection;
sizzling emotional thunderbolts,
after the holidays, reality jolts.
Shedding denial like a bird that molts
feathers from its perceived perfection,
after the holidays, reality jolts
frigid souls into congealed reflection.

Part Four

Verdian Verisimilitude

Nature Endures: Texas Wildflowers in Spring

In Memory of Lady Bird Johnson

Texas hill country in spring look look wildflowers wildflowers
landscape painted with thousands of wildflowers wildflowers
just a short drive out of Austin in springtime fragrant springtime
drive along Market Road 1431 drive on State Highway 2900
feast your eyes on wildflowers every nook and cranny of land
rain lilies sandworts four nerve daisies flax flax everywhere
golden rods Spanish daggers hoop petticoats feast your eyes
lemon paintbrushes bluebonnets so many bluebonnets bluebonnets
wildflowers everywhere just a short drive out of Austin a short
drive grape hyacinths orange jewelweeds heart wing sorrels
so many many Lake LBJ Lake Buchanan surrounded by
wildflowers everywhere desert marigolds coneflowers black
medics bastard cabbage dewberries Texas hill country in spring
landscape painted with thousands of flowers buffalo peas
meadow pinks mountain pinks grass pinks everywhere everywhere
nature endures nature endures nature endures endures endures
wildflowers everywhere Texas hill country in spring wildflowers
wildflowers wildflowers wild wild wild wild wild wild wild

As I View *The Rehearsal* by Degas at the Frick Museum

I'm immediately drawn
back to the summer of '73
when I was just twenty-one
& studied beginning ballet

for several months
at Carnegie Hall no less.
I had a patient teacher
whose vintage name was Amelia.

Ambitious, seeking a big time
showbiz career, my acting
coach proposed I delve
into this rigorous art form

to improve sloppy posture
& gain physical confidence.
Squeezing my thick thighs
into black tights & T-shirt,

wearing new Capezio shoes,
I adored the twice-a-week
basic barre exercises
& all the French terminology

repetitiously repeated:
plié, relevé & assemblé.
How peaceful these classes
hearing the piano accompanist

plunk out Chopin waltzes
andante to allegretto
in the sunlit, mirrored studio.
A stiff physique excelled

at all the graceful positions
from simple first—to fifth.
My great downfall, however,
rhythmic combination steps—

evident my awkward feet
had no talent for syncopation.
Standing behind other students
I looked like a baffled turtle

totally miscast in Swan Lake.
Amelia never patronized or
chided; always professional
with her flaming red locks

parted down the middle
alà—*La Dame aux Camèlias*.
This classical hoofer, who had
grand jetèd all over the world

instinctively knew
I would never make
Rudolph Nureyev a fearful rival—
but she drummed into me

the valuable concept of process
along with daily discipline
as my ligaments began to loosen
becoming miraculously elastic.

About ten or so years ago,
I encountered Madame Amelia
walking on West 57th Street,
her hair thinning with streaks

of whitish-gray, remarkably
still possessing a porcelain visage.
I gleefully reminded her
how she put up with me

three decades past—
& because of her brilliant
pedagogical artistry
I had strong muscular legs

& a healthy spine.
Pretending to slightly recall
my now middle-aged face,
the shrunken woman

inquired about my profession,
peering nostalgically
into somewhat surprised eyes.
Of course, I embellished

a rather flimsy résumé
while she smiled sweetly
truly engaged—as if
she did not want me

to leave or say farewell.
Recently, I read an obituary
that the prima ballerina died
at the age of ninety-seven.

A lifelong vocation
helped preserve her elegant
body, from which consummate
wisdom shaped & developed

so many distinguished dancers.
I can certainly thank
Monsieur Degas for conjuring
this significant chapter in my life

I needed to remember.

How to Create Art If You Can't Draw

Since I'm not Camille Pissarro—
I must paint a church like Saint-Jacques
in my mind. First, the cerebral canvas

will convey a cobalt blue sky
over an impressionistic village
surrounding the mammoth structure

evoking teal-colored stonework.
I visualize this elegant sacred space
a cross between majestic Chartres

and the Gallic glory of Notre Dame.
My artistic brain—not so advanced
to sketch the intricate interior

such as the narthex, nave,
chancel or ornamented chapels.
I'll focus on the detailed exterior

for this fantastical labor of love
with its lancet stained glass
complimenting a Rose window.

I envision my dreamed up cathedral
to have a weathered appearance
out of the 13th Century or before,

with gargoyles & sculpted saints
above arched portals
worthy of a Pope's visit. Also,

similar to an old master drawing,
I'll add a castle-like bell tower
connected to the south transept

(which architectural purists
would most likely scorn)
along with figures of pilgrims

wearing peasant attire
treading pebbled paths
leading to their taste of heaven.

I've mish-mashed images
of hybrid houses of worship—
but for the serenity I desire,

the mental art I've sketched
will give momentary peace
as I close my weary eyes

to imagine this made-up
ethereal creation. And of course,
it's definitely located in France.

Viewing Gert Wollheim's *untitled (couple)* from 1926 at The Jewish Museum

How wonderful to be alive
thriving in the Weimar Republic
which has stabilized our existence.
Luckily, many of us survived
the great bloody war—
even though twelve thousand
Jewish soldiers fought & died.
We must now compensate
for wasted years living in fear.
Happily, the art & music scene
flourishes, the broken economy
resuscitated with new industry
fueling a rich theatrical vibrancy.
Fancy men dress like silent
cinema stars, gaily decked out
in top hats & tuxedos;
women wear pants with bob cut hair
mimicking Louise Brooks.
Vodka or sparkling champagne
is gulped each night at a cabaret
as we lustily foxtrot till sunrise
laughing at our daft decadence.
After all, life could never get worse
than what we've endured—
it could never get worse.
Horror passed & we breathe joy.
Let's really be naughty naughty
& party party with wild abandon.
Pour the drinks & heartily sing:
Wir sind oben auf der welt.
We're on top of the world.

A Fifteenth Century Monk Laments His Vocation
Illuminating Manuscripts

It is the frigid monastery room
where my bony fingers paint away
day after day—I most despise.
After Matins in the stained glass chapel

and cold gruel in the refectory,
I sit before this hard stone table
hunched back for hours
grasping my hog bristle brush

as I dip ultramarine pigments
coloring the Virgin Mary's cursive robe
with touches of sunburnt vermillion
contrasting the ivory holiness

of a fleshy face. It's an ordeal
to capture those immaculate lips
a crack-of-dawn pink, complimenting
her wimpled head with blue veil.

My worn eyeballs
glitter with gold leaf dust
causing watery tears to drip
on vellum—which has the foulest odor

I have grown to passionately hate
since it irritates my sensitive nostrils
with smells of dead animal skins.
I'm always stressed—in a mad frenzy

for the portrait to be reasonably
perfect, so that the finicky scribes
who first copied the inked text
might impress a pretentious Medici.

Such tedium challenges my faith
and I wonder if I still believe
any of this sacred mythology
rushing to finish as daylight fades.

Broken Heart of Operatic Proportion

Like Dido, I mourn
my lost Aeneas;
my mood more Berlioz

than Purcell. The Englishman
withers her away
with a slow lament of death.

The Frenchman lets her scream
in anguish, *"Je vais mourir!"*
Since my lover fled,

my Carthaginian soul
manifested a fall of Troy
in every corpuscle

flowing though these
opera queen veins.
Only months before,

a man with a heroic face
appeared unannounced—
entered my walled world

as curiously as
a wooden horse. We kissed
like naked gods

frockliking in lusty meadows.
Our new romance
raced along

with the lightning speed
of Hermes' winged feet—
until, in a surprise attack

by his own spears of
intimacy fear,
he bolted swiftly

as he had come,
my entire being
pierced by daggers

of rejection—
leaving me shocked
like Hecuba must have been

discovering soldiers
pillaging her ancient city.
Alas, tis finished, it is over.

Up in smoke
this ravaged relationship
burns, ignited—as if on

a fantasized funeral pyre.
As the curtain descends
on my grand tragedy,

flames of despair
engulf my afflicted heart
singing high E-flat

above chorus and orchestra
like a devastated diva,
while memories float back

to celebratory occasions of love.

Insomnia

Toss & turn
in slithery darkness

unable to conjure
sweet dreams

to distract from the dread
of this nightly ritual

lying in my solitary bed.
I ask my virtual companion

Alexa—to please play BBC
Radio, live from London

becoming my newsy lullaby
as I try to nod out

& get shut-eye
only to be cerebrally stimulated

by the grim tragedies
of the day. At some point

during werewolf hours
around three-in-the-morn

I escape into slumber mode
so anxiously desired.

And then, hellish nightmares
begin badgering

my thin as meringue
rest, while brain waves

like tiny lightning bolts
send microscopic cranium

shocks—loosening horrors
tucked inside

an agitated head.
What's worse?

To sleep or not to sleep?
That becomes my nocturnal question.

A Visit From the Ghost of Ruth Gordon

"Never give up, and never under any circumstances face the facts."
—Ruth Gordon

"You've returned from the grave," I exclaimed—
bleary-eyed in bed—waking out of sleep.
Before me, a diaphanous spirit. "Creep
closer—blessed Harold's Maude. I'm ashamed

to confess: I gave up, myself to blame."
Sweetie-pie, I'm not back to chide. Leap
forth! Let these words into your noggin seep.
Listen to sage wisdom. Heed this dead dame.

I inspired you when you were twenty-one,
yet, you've become an aimless automaton.
Commit yourself to youthful dreams again.
For me, my fame came late without regrets.

Get off your ass, remarry theater, then—
risk all for art. Fret not your past upsets.

The Last Frontier Is Not On My Bucket List

When I think of Alaska, Jack London
comes to mind. His book, *The Call of the Wild*
features Buck the sled dog—& beguiled
Yukon prospectors seeking golden fun.
Of course, it's Canada, but the mind reruns
images I've confused with Alaska. Mild
weather didn't exist—when as a child
I viewed brochures picturing moose under
snowy skies. The forty-ninth state looked cold.
Although they say it's environmental
heaven, with glorious mountains to behold,
I doubt I'll visit this land with winter dark
& forests of Sitka spruce so transcendental.
When I need trees, I'll hike to Central Park.

My Brush with Genius

In Memory of Edward Albee

"You are the American Dream,"
scripted lines spoken by Grandma
to a muscular young man
penetrating my unworldly ears

as I sat transfixed
watching this absurd comedy
The American Dream
in an amateur theatre

production, terrified
of my nascent puberty—
numb with pangs
of inherent aloneness

within the closeted world
of my adolescence.
Mister Edward Albee,
your artful words

have resonated
like an echo chamber
for over a half century
haunting my turbulent mind.

You, a fellow homosexual,
a prophetic dramatist
whose razor-sharp writing
strips to bare bones

the rawest emotions
of the fractured
human condition.
Your profound plays

scream bloodcurdling rage
peppered with wry wit
& wicked humor
illuminating audiences

by scathing observations
of the meaningless farces
challenging a narcissistic
dumbed down society

lost in deep denial
of its egocentric values.
I once encountered you
butt naked

in a YMCA locker room.
You had just showered
as I timidly approached
announcing: "I played Daddy

in your one act, *The Sandbox,*
at a high school drama festival."
You glared back at me
a surprised look

of bemused/annoyance
replying, "I'm glad you did that."
Yes, hallowed playwright—
I'm glad I did that too.

Time Travel

Why do I always long for days of yore?
Why such a sourpuss for the present?
In the past, did the world offer much more,

or, is it just mental myths I yearn for?
When losing luck's lottery, I rage, vent
like thunderbolt Thor, Norse god from days of yore—

blotting out weathered failures from before—
denying truths conjuring the unpleasant.
Think back: Did the world ever offer much more?

Childhood, bullied blue, rarely peaceful, nor
teen years: great angst as an adolescent.
And yet, I always long for days of yore—

damming what I became, sometimes deplore.
Life could have been this or that, but wasn't.
Awake! When did the world offer much more?

Time to release—*should have been,* lock the door
to cobwebbed closets, stashed with deep regrets.
Why do I always long for days of yore?
In the past, did the world (really) offer much more?

A Villanelle for the Liturgical Season of Lent

We are dust, and to dust we shall return—
words chanted in churches on Ash Wednesday.
Yet, for most of us, we never quite learn

to praise quotidian days, to discern
gospel truth from pious claptrap, as we say
we are dust, and to dust we shall return.

In our lust for success, we connive, burn
bridges with foes, insist: Do It My Way!
New paths are lost to us. We never quite learn

to swallow pride, offer heartfelt amends, earn
forgiveness from estranged kin. As hair grays
we are dust, and to dust we shall return

eludes us. We grieve over failed dreams, turn
bitter, cursing Yahweh at our dismay.
If only—most of us could ever learn

time on earth, just an eye's blink; cease yearnings
for gold calves, idols of our mortal stay.
We are dust, and to dust we shall return—
yet, for most of us, we never quite learn.

Not so Clear-Eyed

For Mary Ann Caffery

"I think I'm in the early stages
of Fuchs dystrophy," my sister whines
over long distance. "It's a degenerative

eye disease, affecting the endothelium
which maintains proper
fluid in the cornea." A mouthful

for my scrambled brain
to absorb through cell phone
static. "And by the way,

my ophthalmologist
tells me, you'll probably
develop this condition too—

it's highly genetic."
Perhaps that explains
the blinding glare

magnifying morning light
as I walk to buy the newspaper
at the newsstand. Or the rainbows

around red lights & streetlights
glimmering after dark. Or the
squinty impressionistic vision

I experience on awakening
most days, until the ashen
cloudiness dissipates.

Just one more misery
to list on my long list
of daily worries

about future aging issues.
At the Frick Museum, I ponder
J. M. W. Turner's watercolor,

Chateau de Dieppe. A fusion of
delicate pink & blue pastels
dominated by radiant sunglow

as if this French port city
was being cleansed & redeemed
by hallowed beams from heaven.

Brown etchings of structures
faintly emerge through splashed
brush strokes of luminous white;

a lone castle on a hill
looms vaguely, almost formless
through the abstract atmosphere

painted on paper. I wonder
if the artist was suffering
from Fuchs dystrophy too?

Caught on Television

For Joseph Christopher Molloy

We saw you on the Yankees Channel
on a muggy Sunday afternoon
when the Bombers played the Jays
& both teams sweated bullets
competing on the field of dreams
while spitting saliva & chewing
Double Bubble Bubble Gum.
And then unexpectedly—
it happened; the camera man
panned on your poker face
in the not-so-private dugout
as you slid your index finger
into your right nasal cavity
thinking—no one was looking—
turning that bony limb
back & forth with vigor
clearing a clogged nostril
just above those uptight lips.

Dear Manager of the Pinstripes,
you were anything but alone
while fans watching intently
from comfortable living rooms
witnessed you digging away
as we collectively shouted at TVs—
"Don't pick your nose Aaron Boone!"

Remember, O descendent of Daniel,
during the middle of a baseball game
you might not be able to see us,
but—we certainly can see you.

Standing in Line at the Post Office

We wait & wait & wait & wait
just to buy a couple of stamps.
Curt postal clerks infuriate—
dawdling—while we wearily wait.
Cool deportments disintegrate
as feet & legs throb with cramps.
We wait & wait & wait & wait
just to buy a couple of stamps.

A Worn Out Queer's *Der Rosenkavalier*

For Renée Fleming

Why is the cock crowing at this hour
rather than a less nightmarish moment?
It nags this old man to rise. I'm so bent
out of shape in dark morning, a dour
drab, horror face homo, bitterly sour
to all near, in anguished disagreement
with an aging body, lacking a glint
of spark in glazed eyes. I'm Mister Glower.
And yet, there was a remarkable time
decades ago, when I bounced out of bed
as if a dancer in a famed ballet troupe—
limbs agile, my fresh countenance sublime.
Like Strauss's Marschallin, I feel such dread
aware my youthful prime—I'll never recoup.

Self-Portrait of an Aging Southern Opera Queen

I am the creative spirit's humble instrument…
—Arturo Colautti
Translated by Glen Sauls

All Southerners are born of tragedy. It's a well known
fact in Dixie. Ask anyone from below the line,
they'll tell you the same thing:

Blanche Dubois was undoubtedly
one of our more stable kinfolk. That's why
my vulnerable visage

reflects a lingering loss
lodged in sky-blue eyes: giving my face
the only feature called—handsome.

Salvation from the curse of the birth
occurred in the Crescent City
as my adolescent ears

became emancipated
by the ebony goddess, Leontyne Price,
singing Adriana Lecouvrer's lyrical credo

Io son l'umile ancella, del genio creator—

freeing my soul to flee forever.
The Northern sojourn—has been unkind
to my magnolia skin, its lambent glow

lost along with rhapsodic dreams—
faded in turbulent times
like memories of an unrequited love.

Survival in the Yankee carnival
necessitated menial servitude, etched
wrinkles on a once hopeful Harlequin

now relinquishing gray hair
from the electric shock of the drama.
An imaginary garland of gardenias

adorns my balding crown,
giving sweet fragrance
to an old life, whose only

cerebral solace: opera arias
comforting a well-preserved brain—
mantras of Verdian verisimilitude.

About the Author

Davidson Garrett was born in Shreveport, Louisiana, and lives in New York City. He trained for the theater at The American Academy of Dramatic Arts and graduated from The City College of New York with an M.S. in Education. A member of SAG/AFTRA and Actors Equity, he worked in theater, television, and film for several years. His poetry has been published in many periodicals and literary journals including, *The New York Times, The Episcopal New Yorker, Xavier Review* from New Orleans, *The Stillwater Review, 2 Bridges Review, First Literary Review East, Sensations Magazine, Impossible Archetype, The Ekphrastic Review,* and in *Podium,* the literary journal of the 92nd Street Y. Davidson is the author of the poetry collection, *King Lear of the Taxi,* published by Advent Purple Press, the chapbook, *To Tell the Truth I Wanted to be Kitty Carlisle and Other Poems,* published by Finishing Line Press, the chapbooks, *Southern Low Protestant Departure: A Funeral Poem,* and *What Happened to the Man Who Taught Me Beowulf and Other Poems,* both published by Advent Purple Press. A Pushcart Prize nominee, Davidson drove a yellow taxi for forty years to subsidize his artistic pursuits.

Made in the USA
Columbia, SC
09 November 2020